F
B

MACULAR HOLE

CATHERINE WAGNER

Published in the United States by

Fence Books
303 East Eighth Street, #B1
New York, NY 10009
www.fencebooks.com

Book design by

Rebecca Wolff

Fence Books are distributed by

University Press of New England
www.upne.com

Fence Books are printed in Canada by

Westcan Printing Group
www.westcanpg.com

Library of Congress Cataloguing in Publication Data
    Wagner, Catherine [1969–]
    Macular Hole / Catherine Wagner

Library of Congress Control Number: 2003116980

ISBN 0-9740909-1-3

FIRST EDITION
Second Printing

Thanks to the editors of the following magazines and websites that published earlier versions of these poems: *Boston Review, Colorado Review, DC Poetry Anthology, Denver Quarterly, Fence, The Gig, Gutcult, Interim, Kiosk, Pom2, Radical Society, Ribot, Shearsman,* and the *West House Press Anthology* (on www.gutcult.com). "Imitating" was published in 2004 in a Leafe Press chapbook, *Imitating,* as "Exercise 22." The title "For you everywhere Phoebus the fields of song are laid out" is borrowed from the "Hymn to Apollo" in the 2003 Penguin edition of *The Homeric Hymns,* tr. Jules Cashford. Thanks also to the Ragdale Foundation for a residency during which some of these poems were written. The two photos of mailboxes were taken by Martin Corless-Smith; they belong to houseboats moored Thameside in Brentford, London.

TABLE OF CONTENTS

My what to replace my

In an economic game
What would I trade for *my*
my favorite trick
begone! and "I" begone, ballast over the side.

Stand on the concrete sit on the grass.

Whose.

In the name of God and country
give up your name.

In God and country
given up and given.

The hoard of flowers
opened in his side
burrow in
the maculate room
a quiet gigantic fucking

I was eating his side who made me
I burrowed in to invent him further
more and further in
grammatically to please him

in my pleasing dress Damn it

Bled irregularly
and late from the stem
banish it and damned if it's not on the bed
Fasten inside the soft boated blood
a tiny carcass veined all round and eyed
absorption and the dissolute conception
a little self and is not what I am

What demon's come to stick its eyes on you

That was my portion God was all of it
who took it me
Abandoned me flouting in the wood
and branching
sun yellows yellows yells in the gray twigs
I'm not in there
I saw it from out here
I wrote it from later
leaned on a wood thing
greedy as a punch
to make it go like mine

I'm total I'm all I'm absorbed in this meatcake

I gave you a sentence, can't back it with po-lice
Can't back it with any conviction at all

That frees me to say any lie I develop
That frees me of meaning and of consequence

I heard that prayer's efficacious on flowers
Long-distance or local, prayer helps make them grow

I submit that I had better mean what I'm saying
"I'm not the one saying it" "just writing it down"

Well who then is saying it. Trucks in the offing,
finch on the phonewire, movement of tree.

I'm not stupidly assailed by the moonlight
I'm an example, an experimental

Attempt to assess how a kid of my talents
Responds when she's given the life that I was

I'm the control and experiment bothly
you'll never get a result out of me

My guilt is omnipotence erupting backwards
heartbeat spans outward rebuffed at the skin

I'm total I'm all I'm absorbed in this meatcake
If I did all I could you'd shut up/be glad

Like fingers of a hand we all act as one
and aren't always needed, aren't needed as all

The divinity of man

Roseation, spreading, yeastily beering up, the white soft legs and
    the golden hair.
The slits in the chest and the fur skirt. The mountain, the desert.
Sleep for a long time and a thrust of activity: log rolling, fall off
    a skyscraper,
phenomenologues, cigarettes, korn, seeding herpes lip to lip.
Why LSD in the seventies, why coke in the eighties,
why Ecstasy in the nineties, why Ritalin.
To bolster the wandering mind; to bolster the wandering heart
to bolster the glamor; to glamor the wander.
The glamorous self and its story: no can do.

I was at congress with myself

I was at congress with myself to conclude
    should I tax myself, to strengthen my
        reserves and strictly exercise
        myself, so I'll haul myself back up
        if I fall down
    or should I ratchet down the tax, release the lever
        and run outside and see what's there to do
        and give myself a job, or blow it
        on one bamboozle eve extravaganza
the world at night was twitching and flapping out
    from my congress, and I gathered it in and dreamt
  to my outnumberment

I walked in the house

I walked in the house
on the flat aspect of the wood
I took rectangular instruction of the wood

when I walked I turned at the wall
and on the flat I moved steadily

unimpeded, not tumbling, climbing or short of breath.
I walked in ease on the flat.

Something electric charged into our account
and zinged out of it, pre-instructed

and paid for the house. I felt
house on my heel then instep and toe.
I had a bad foot and I paid
to get it fixed so I could walk here.
I paid for the house and I paid for the
foot that touches it. I paid to be
directed rectangularly and down a hall.
I curved my body to direct
my waste through a hole. I am helped
and paying for it.

all of me exchanged,
housing exchange.

          I saw us standing
     up in the world.
And we sank into
   exchange
  vibrating transparency
          like a sea nettle
          afloat in the night sea

the edges of the sea-veil
   tensed slapping above, visible
when the wind crevassed and doilied

               If there is a ceiling to exchange
                    and above it sky
          I don't can't see it and I don't know why
                    I want it
               above my house which is crystalline gel edges

     because the whole world's disappeared
                         viewed as exchange

I broke my arm and the window
integrally to exchange.

I paid someone to fix me and improve
the window, triple-glazing it, and warmer
I rebounded   knit in knit up.
All parties to the event's aftermath
                    were paid.

Suppose I did not go in pain
                    to hospital, did not visit and revisit
for x-rays, left the window smashed
                    and sat here by it,
          stuck up
                    ugly among the crystalline
                              and cold.
I was painful and determined
not to play, and with the other unemployed

weighed—

    the ghostship
sagged with holes.

            —So you want to be a thing outside exchange?

           Drain out the dying bath
           see what color you are?

The coin changed hands

identical   with a will
to transact.

Kill so we feel safe and comfortable

This is called the Mississippi mash, this kind of kick—leg up,
foot smashed against both sides opponent's head,
or spinneret, foot comes round your body
turning backward fast, and hooks 'em.
Squeezed tight between my legs
so we feel safe and comfortable.
Who's my fucker? Who will be my special fucker?

Freely esposa

Right now he is with the guys.

They are not talking about us.
They are eating and competing
to be funny
—"I will not laugh,
I will not laugh, as I risk this joke."

Why can you not be funny and
laugh at your own jokes?

You own the conversation if you don't.

How to fix him: do not laugh at the expected moment.

> Dating Advice: [I love you.]
> Drink to assuage embarrassment.
> Kiss him and turn your face away and put your face in
>   your hands.
> Then smack him.

I can say this misanthropy because men are not misogynistic now.

* * *

A human is shaped like a cock
under the billowing blue sky.
A cock without a man
isn't going to plug anybody and relax.

This metaphor explains everything.
It explains the veins on my tits.

* * *

A bathroom clean before a party
glare like it's never used
They will think I wipe
They will think I'm nice
my platform gleaming
the people who pee in my
house look at our towels the
corners are flush

Clean and careful and merry

Give the woman a pedestal
bouncy pedestal bingbong
my ring rang on

* * *

This is black and goes all the way back
This is blue is your pee in a wave
This is a sink where you wash a platter
and curl up on it to save
under stretched plastic your matter

The indifferent sofa abducted space
I fell asleep here

* * *

Wrote a rune for my pigtails
For the straight back part I made today
First time
By following a tendon with the comb:

Hair on both sides
Goes to the end
Of a gathering of hair
That smells like my house
And then a lot of air
On both sides
And all among
The dead and little eggs
Laid invisible
All over me

Wrought in filigree and wrought in granite

Two fingers of plot: Wrought in Filigree and Wrought in Granite.

Wrought in Granite is set on the sea. The sea is dark and light-mottled and massive, resembles granite and tortuously recomposing and veined with heat. Authoritarian. Enter the hot tiny bay. Flicker light and acrid smell of cooking, feel choked, as if inside an onion. In the morning they were a slave ship, in the afternoon they were a mother ship, in the evening a whore ship. They were women and they swam ashore.

Wrought in Filigree is a thin boy with a gay heart and a scared face, white-eyelashed, crawling through a barbed wire fence.

Scary ballad

My eat, little girl, like a bed collapsed in
My eat nervous like for your life
And when the pie was opened
What a pretty
Sandpaper bird
Yellow cloth hole in the ocean
Rash skinny song and a dancing man
That was the cord I held

Who gave that little girl cold medicine to eat
My thighbruise made up to look pink
Nobody knew because nobody saw
Everyone walk down the street

Song

He cannot ask for compliments
and oh how he desires them
a cancered, greentoothed, bawdy boy
sad eyes to recommend him

You can ask, you can ask
the magic glamors and shatters
you can ask, you can ask
the sweet liquor flares up in the furnace

A dog asks for affection
I bend down like a queen
my mother nervous, heels and lace
I tell her "you look fine"

When you ask, when you ask
you pull back the healing scab
you permit the lie, you drain the bath
you air the unsealed meat

A bash, and I wanna look good

Stick body dump body crank body crack bod
Oh, ho, blow the man down
Give me a rhyme to blow the man down

A monster to be with a monster to see
Oh, ho, blow the man down
A canker on one lip a bruise on my knee
Give me a rhyme to blow the man down

I told you I'm ugly and I'll tell you why
Oh, ho, blow the man down
I saw you today and you looked mighty fine
Give me a rhyme to blow the man down

If you looked like horse and I thought you were cool
Oh, ho, blow the man down
I'd want you beside me use you for a fool
Give me a rhyme to blow the man down

Scary so scary scarier than your lives
Oh, ho, blow the man down
A day like a thing on a fork it arrives
Give me a rhyme to blow the man down

At Newark Airport my man has arrived
Oh, ho, blow the man down
Derived from the plane in a tangible hide
Give me a rhyme to blow the man down

Some days mine is saggy some days it is torn
Oh, ho, blow the man down
Some days it's a fine fit I'll give you the horn
Give me a rhyme to blow the man down

San Francisco ballad

Dear boys there is a socket
I have a problem
there is a plug
I have a problem

> *Sh shh s'okay s'okay*
> *Come inside away from me*

there is a trench
there is a festive grape
there is a sodden log
there is a mistake

> *Sh shh s'okay s'okay*
> *Come inside away from me*

Now I'm going to sleep in the warm
Green in the blades

> *Sh shh s'okay s'okay*
> *Come inside away from me*

Dear boys my limb incognito clean
my radiant nerve clang clean

> *Sh shh s'okay s'okay*
> *Come inside away from me*

An hendy hap

I saw the tyrant in the bath
his thing waved like anemone
The chesthair draggled
sprang to curl
he stood to dry himself.

Here is a perfect circle hedge of bronze
and when I stand here not afraid
in sweet consent and ritual
upbraid me through the vein that feeds the tumor
and pinch me off, the tumor hot and gorged
dried now to scab.

An eyelid like a wafer
concave and hardening.

And when I woke
and walked between the two trees to my house,
the house they'd lent me,
the door was blown open
I saw that I was single
and my marriage capillaried clasped to all
to the field and the brown world
I saw it to the tracks
a thousand stalks of canegrass downed by snow

frazzled the field in pointing yellow
pointing everywhere
some of them stood up
some of them pronged through by the next stalks
not mirth or death
it doesn't mean anything to point.

There was a place in the brain, a red knot

My tiny babycrat
Loose in a pool and dying
My tiny cat
Is hanged up and a-dying
My little bracelet
Bangs on the page
My proud babycrat
Smut-faced in its rage
Go away little dogface
Go away little phage
I'm driving up to Providence
Investigate the gauge
My speed is like I pass 'em all
I don't pass anyone
Singing hard I give 'em hell
I sing 'em down the drain

Delver, light a match to flare the stink
and tell me why you are so bad.
Are you the scourge of God?
    The author has bad thoughts not me.

Delver, what is sexual?
    Sexual is the secret and uncontained.

Why am I happy?
>*Everyone is nice to you.*

Delver, I have no more questions. What is wrong?
>*It wasn't the id it was what they wanted you to do.*
>*The mass grave morphs into uranium you have millions!*
>*Whistle through the caverns and steeples, the school*
>*and the bright columnar people   people gone.*

I walk left and abort my future.
Turn right and pow a new world.
The past flew up my crotch and infested my brain.
I birthed a big one.

Big bang

A splat of mud and stones electrolaced
Began to crawl.

Somersaulted out on a cord of blood
Hit a climax of discomfiture
And recomposed itself to rot.

Make me an animal better than that.

Who admitted you?

My mother
I was fucked for
a coupling inside of that inside her
a split and crack and grotesque growthery
a veiny fish and limbs alarming off
and thrash her good
and split her out, a yellow wrinkling

Song: Scary several light

Once on Hays Street
Walking home in darkness
Saw car lights pass
Saw fence posts drive out and conquer
Black stripes pulsing over house
Over lawns and house

There was Wagner
Fearful walking
Saw the light split
By the driving ranks of
Shadows
Marching in the several light
The scary several light

Here is Wagner
Swaying in the hammock
Cover one big toe
Up with the other toe
Dying
In the scary several light

Here comes baby
Screaming down vagina
Brain tissue coning
Making of himself a painful
Squeeze-toy
In the scary several light
The scary several light

Afternoon
The light diffuses
Cramps around the hammock
Cramps around my eyeballs
Rolls hugely
Tightly, hugely from the sky
The mottled blooming light

Here's a curio
Dangling in the hammock
No one sees my folded legs
Touch no world-surface but hammock
In the opportunity light
The several daytime light

I call on creatures
Living in the sky today
I adjure you
Emerge and dive your wings and bodies
Prevail across the scary light
Cavernous several light

Writing my poem
All about the several light
When the phone rings
Alerting me to the car noises
Ignored them in the several light
Sound-adjusted light

Check the message
6:38 p.m.
It's my mother
Checking on the progress of the baby
Wrestling in the dim water
The scary several light

Perfect love

Today Ambrose rolled over for the first time since in the pub
with Damaris and Adam; twice today. Also, he objected when I
tried to take away my waterbottle.

And, I will love my fellow people with a perfect love.

Working for another until one is more than exhausted
is not the same as having perfect love for him.

I hate the baby, stop crying.
I hate you and put you down.
I hate you coming over my life like a bag.

Inside the bag
a garden bigger than the inside of my eye
high protective walls
invisibles twitching and uncovering themselves

I made that up so no one will take the baby away
anyway, sometimes thus and sometimes
choked down in the hard tight bag.

The imprisoner is time, or my sense of it.
A great suction fattens
on my trés rich hours.

My hours
are not mine and
more.

So I write a moralizing poem
so a poem to feel better.
Do what I want to it.
Go back and prune it, and hope
the E in it whangs harder
inside the smaller cell.
My child can whang unpruned – no, I'm espaliering him. Can't
        help that.

Everyone was born inside a bag
and came out here, to a bag of atmosphere
and satellites where we'll live inside cool greenhouse plastic
when the world is too hot.
 Inside a bag my son will go to live
he can look down here to the fried-up
water and say, Fuck you for driving so much
and fuck you for crying, and look at
the inside of our bag! It's all vines.

He can have vines because I can't drink wine
while I'm breastfeeding.
Tyrant. Asleep and saying huu,
fantastic waxen kicking
figurine, like a kick in the head, little

fat bag, a good drug
I see more of the
him in.

Inmost

Skin. Outside of that: house → town → atmosphere →
sky emptied and lit up from inside.
Skin → womb → amniotic sac →
inmost, the dividing baby.
I am predicted to have one by my insides.
Inmost, awaiting.   There we go.
Inmost, a bit of foam.
Inmost grew me out to hold it.
Ah, fuck. Inmost came out.
I saw the mailbox 'Inmost.' Sent the letter.
Formally—I thought not of it. From inside I had
the baby, nothing formal about it. I didn't structure it.
From outside I had the baby and was stunned
to find it outermost, most obvious among things boundaried.

For you everywhere Phoebus the fields of song are laid out

The rowers of the evening don't get up early to row.
The rowers of the evening pass and the guy on the next bench looked at me.
Look away, dickie man.
If I were cruel and smashed your head. Or baby's, which I could barely write.
The baby has a head of glass and I will let it be. A pencil end
Stabbed him from between the sofa cushions and he bled.
He was blown and glowed with milk. The milk made him alive.
I walked down to the river and returned and found him still alive.
I returned and he was crying shaky and alive.
His father fed him from a bottle and I fed him from a fat skin flask.
My blood made blood and his blood made blood to fill him.
He was bigger and his bag packed peach.
I he looked around. He sucked, which looks like chewing on my breast.
More me was available. He loved it. More him too, he looked upon his head of glass.
Then the water was too flashy with reflection. Saltwater from his eyes of glass.
Scull on the river upside down and right side up.

Imitating

(UT, ID, OR, WA, CA, NV November 2001)

H atred and doom

Took it torquing jealous into my gut. I flamed
& I came kindness.
I hoped I was kind and good and fretted
my tongue with pink & raw serrations.
I imitated nobody in
          my hate.
I was alone.

I harnessed my powers

& graphed onto

the ranks of trees   onto the
army sergeants
the prickle close-
cropped
+++++++++++++++++++

I was trying to
pie myself
comfortably
so I would be delicious
& secure in my shell.

A Song

> *Nothing to grieve about*
> *nothing to do*
> *no one to save*
> *I love you*
>
> *and I don't care how hurt*
> *you get.*

My dear treasure
gold pitted wicked
center
ladling grim of the heart
splat shit treasure
    splatted on my shirt
& burned myself.

I didn't have time not to burn myself
the trajectory of the pan too important
& I fucked it up
   opening myself to its importance
I did not defend myself
I fucked it up
onto the floor
my raisin role,
& the floor
was totally impassive.
I knew I would scream if I didn't write it down because I needed
   to be alone reproducing.

I wasn't imitating

I danced in the back of the car
danced my feet on the roof.
Happy.
What is happy.
Energy for now & for the next thing
It IS CAPABILITY
I can be in the back of the car, it is my house
open-grated
speed
my friends live in my house
they move my house

My mettle

is ruffled & standing straight up
it's brusquely
strictly up my spine,
which is fun,
& means I could
  eat or east
  anybody
who tried to kiss my mouth.
I could east or west
 them because of my mettle
& I wouldn't be imitating
anybody.
I might be imitating the radio or the egg I ate
but I was breakfasted
in the miracle spreading out
    above my head
& moving its center over
someone else's head

I was jealous & flew at the person & the
miracle bewitched me

I soaped myself & presented

myself in a   soft light

a breathing light
    I would thank you
    for embracing me
& your head, then I was pushing away on your head with my
feet into a huge bright horse I was inside of,

& I knew I was imitating, because my legs could make no
gestures that had not already been made. Why was I writing so
much? Because I was impressed, & saddled up & ridden.

God was not personal to me

God would become personal to me when I
thought I was so sexy

which was craven.

God was neither personal nor impersonal, it was a
questionnaire.

I drew a picture for the questionnaire
of a man in flared
    trousers, & there was
      me, wearing a fuckable mighty.   That was my answer.

The questions were inside
      like candy.
Passing "Salmon la Sac"

M
y greed was outrageous
power-outageous

I felt all better & feverish
my braincase was
hypertranslucent
& exercised with rumpling
tumbling skin
which I held gently
over my brain
like a blanket
or a weird threat
of cutting it off
from the world.
Oh my god. My
chest got cut off in
the mine.
I was mine & I was going
to dig myself a jewel.
I dug a little bone in me
I dug a little boneshaped
hole in me, I loved it
Hello you fuckers!
Dug around in there making
my emergencies go off

I thought they were lovebells
  or runaway truck ramps

I'm hungry.

Felt so alert I was frightened

had to keep my eyes open really wide

+ * + * + * + * + * + * + * + * + * +

now slowed to research

Coming toward me

for Frankie

Polar bears floating toward me
and red race-cars with silver grills vrumming toward me
and soft green passages and blurry lemon highlights
diagonals squares and cradles
of indeterminate color are coming toward me
an astronaut shape with a red round opaque glass mask
rises up toward me and falls beneath the horizon
which is below the bones of my cheeks
or below my lower eyelids or below me
I have recently masturbated and hair-sparklings
descend before me to reward me
and warmth and shut eyes
teeth or soft or ladies
peeking from large black wigs, tiny heads
wires and pathways
I could not show to anyone or sell
though feathery and mottled gray and sailing
in a ricocheting re-angling of sail

Not very much is abstracted

which means pulling strands gummily into a word or system
that breaks them off into itself.

Here is an equals sign who stands in sun
like an abstract mess. I did not do myself.
I did not brush or comb my hair. I did not rid
red blotches round my nose. Everyone saw
coursing round the rim of icy intersectual
rim of me. I wrote a daring song I didn't know
to plaster/use my teeth I didn't know to simply break it off, the
rest of the song would heal over.

Allied with it were all receptacles

A mailbox doesn't change what it takes in.
The mail arrives if crumpled in integral state.

I wrap what I take in
and ject it out objectified.
This pleasure is a mighty wine
to turn the outward in, unfurl it

realigned until the corners match
my corners. I do so without thinking

in my thinking. Who is alert enough
to watch the corner while it vamps and shudders

repositioning the being hall as bright and deep

or fantastically dismembered
walls of animal?
The food inside my breast
needed a needer.

Spatchcocked boy, broken in transmission

The reward for buying
Is the bought thing.
Lasts awhile
Starts to look old.
I desired a market for me
In my bought boy.
Sat up straight
To sell my body better
Needed to wash my hair
When I got home
I bought him again without
Trying. At my breast
He sold himself
To me as my
Needer. My valuable purse
Turned outside and walks
In danger on the road.

Macular hole

Please god love me and buy me

Read this hillock and ride me
Wraith typing all day for money.

God bought me today for two silver fish in a can
God bought me tomorrow for bland in a pan
and a card an email from Rebecca

Bought four hours of my control alt delete shut down
Bought a new day-section with a headstand

My commerce in shall

Sky like a grandstand
Transact

God performed me today for a half minute
lucky
in locker room hiding my boobs from the kids
and my hair is silky and my mane shot silk gold

Bought a book on economy
Georgie Bataille
Called about plane tickets
Georgie Bataille
I bought my debt today
Georgie Bataille hooray
Debt off my God today

God off my debt in a macular hole

I dream of an end like a fount to this night
Run thinner and thinner and then it's all light
Macerated in signal

by my go

I bought my ghost I walk my ghost

I don't believe in bodiless

Who cannot say
A thing without
Lying.

Levee

Extending the
Hinged yardstick out
To measure downward in a yellow arc
The air is as long as the measuring rod
Plus whatever I have not measured.
If I stand at the end of the measuring
Pull the measure to me
And extend it again I have
Gone away.
I stood behind a frozen waterfall
inside a dam in Baltimore.
Many sons
pushed out between many legs.
A waterfall is stable
photographable
and goodbye goodbye goodbye.

I awake possessed by God

and annex the darting mind
to replace it and make it know
flung up in a dishtowel
with a sweater fuzzing out of my skirt

But what should I obey or own
if I swallow my sense and my sword
in a great throbbing beating in my face?

Resume, face

It's dirty
looking   and it
won't come off. It has sun in it

the dirt rolling into me
      until I'm aerated and mud.
blastules cornering me, blastopores
            excreting in me

The tiny limbs of veins
didn't grow out of me into the earth
            till I died
when I did not look at myself at all.

It's like we'll be together forever
            so why should we talk. It's like parents.

      As looking at yellow mountains
            against blue sky. They're flaming
      and it is your eyes.

The violent career of God

The sky resembles something
with something behind it.

That's the fascination
of the snowglobe

or bottle-garden.
I net the snow the fence the bean-tree wall

glancing.

*

And to remove myself from scene
I flew outside sky.

To re-enact the effort of my thought
I left the house

and retroactive slammed transcendence
inside metaphor.

Trying to walk out of there. You can't.

*

And I alone escaped
and did a thing again

covered a dark patch on my face with cream.

*

God presided president and replaced god.
I was grown again out of my eyes

in skin, and covered up the past.
I am a glamorous blistering garment

and poisoned the strong world.
On the rooftop 5 hilly gardens of moss

and what among the brown
a furor hid secret from me.

Induce

Introduce the boat to the water.
The boat's a house and won't go anywhere.

The water abandons the boat at the top of the water, at water level.

The water also abandons itself at the top of itself.

Then my son, and his mouth-corners
out and up; he dazzles.
He came to me to eat.

The water abandoned itself back toward the sea,
left the boat in a muck

and rocked and rummaged it up again, in some hours;
the river was tidal.

The water abandoned its muck in a line on the boat
and borrowed its paint.

The milk abandons me but I don't want it. He may as well have it.
The boat could do nothing to the water; it dents the water.

The water flees and recovers, and plays with the hole in itself. It's brilliant.

The inverse of the hole was a house.

The boat was called Induce. It made some people
up and down, up and down, and a hole in the water.

FENCE ⋑ BOOKS

A biannual journal of poetry, fiction, art and criticism, *Fence* has a mission to redefine the terms of accessibility by publishing challenging writing distinguished by idiosyncrasy and intelligence rather than by allegiance with camps, schools, or cliques. *Fence* has published works by some of the most esteemed contemporary writers as well as excellent writing by complete unknowns. It is part of our mission to support writers who might otherwise have difficulty being recognized because their work doesn't answer to either the mainstream or to recognizable modes of experimentation.

Fence Books is an extension of that mission: With our books we provide exposure to poets and writers whose work is challenging and self-determined. **The Alberta Prize** is an annual series administered by Fence Books in collaboration with the Alberta duPont Bonsal Foundation. The Alberta Prize offers publication of a first or second book of poems by a woman, as well as a five thousand dollar cash prize.

Our second prize series is the **Fence Modern Poets Series**. This contest is open to poets of either gender and at any stage in their career, and offers a one thousand dollar cash prize in addition to book publication.

For more information about either prize, visit our website at **www.fencebooks.com**, or send an SASE to: Fence Books/[Name of Prize], 303 East Eighth Street, #B1, New York, New York, 10009.

For more about *Fence,* visit **www.fencemag.com**.

Fence Books Titles

MACULAR HOLE   Catherine Wagner

THE OPENING QUESTION   Prageeta Sharma
                              2004 FENCE MODERN POETS SERIES

Sky Girl   Rosemary Griggs
                                      2003 ALBERTA PRIZE

Nota   Martin Corless-Smith

APPREHEND   Elizabeth Robinson
                              2003 FENCE MODERN POETS SERIES

Father of Noise   Anthony McCann

The Real Moon of Poetry and Other Poems   Tina Brown Celona
                                      2002 ALBERTA PRIZE

The Red Bird   Joyelle McSweeney
                              2002 FENCE MODERN POETS SERIES

Can You Relax in My House   Michael Earl Craig

ZIRCONIA   Chelsey Minnis
                                      2001 ALBERTA PRIZE

MISS AMERICA   Catherine Wagner